The Light
In The Devil's Tavern

Elizabeth Mooney

Nightengale Press

The Light In The Devil's Tavern

©2024 Elizabeth Mooney

Library of Congress Cataloging-in-Publication Data
Mooney, Elizabeth
The Light in the Devil's Tavern/ Elizabeth Mooney
ISBN 13: 978-1-945257-47-6
Genre: Inspirational

Published in the United States of America
©2024
Nightengale Press
www.nightengalepress.com

February 2024
10 9 8 7 6 5 4 3 2 1

TO
Amy,
Thank you for your
support { Keep shining :
        Keep smiling}

The Light
In The Devil's Tavern

Be Still.
Be Peace.
Be Present
Be love.

Love.

XO

PROLOGUE

I was in so much pain. My groin throbbed. I discovered a lump in my thigh. My digestive system was off. I wasn't sleeping. My anxiety was rampant.

I needed to turn the focus back on myself and away from all the drama. It was affecting me not only emotionally, but mentally and physically. As a self-proclaimed control freak and a hypochondriac with OCD, I didn't know how to handle this debilitating pain. I went for blood work, changed my diet and exercise routine, and loaded up on antibiotics. My IBS flared up. The stress consumed my nervous system. It was one cluster fuck after the next.

"I am done. I am tired of this. I surrender," I said to God and to the Universe.

Finally, one of the millions of doctors I was seeing recommended a homeopathic chiropractor. I joined a meditation practice.

At my first session, I was taught, "Release the fear." Far easier said than done. That fear was like a weighted blanket, both holding me down and comforting me for way longer than it should.

What if it all works out? What if everything's OKAY?

Release the fear, and let love in.

It took some time, but once that release came, I finally fell in love…with my soul. I surrendered the fear and the need to control all outcomes. My whole heart opened, and I became love.

I truly believe God continued putting me in these chaotic, challenging, devastating situations because I wasn't learning. I wasn't trusting.

As an empath, I'd been given the gift of reading, knowing, and feeling energy, but I was too stuck in my own way. I allowed other people's energy to block my gifts, derailing me on my road to happiness. I had to clear the path of these energy vampires.

This book is a reflection on that journey, on the many, many people and situations that led me to that moment of surrender. As I learned to identify my insecurities, my strengths, and my weaknesses, I found a way for them to fuel me instead of taking me down. They ignited my fire, my passions, and most importantly, they served a purpose.

Writing down these stories marks an ending. And every ending paves the way for a brand new beginning.

This book is dedicated
to my daughter, Danika.

May your light always shine
even when it makes
others uncomfortable.

May your happiness be a beacon
to others and bring smiles
to strangers' faces.

May your presence be known –
with love for yourself and for others.

Remember, you are a "lucky girl."
You are love!

Run amongst the wild horses
and live with abandon.

You are protected, my love.

Love,
Your Momma

1
BEGIN

I'm the oldest child and the only girl in a traditional Italian-American/Irish family from Long Island, New York. I have two younger brothers, Tom and Matt, a father who was relatively absent both physically and emotionally due to work, and a mother who often left me in charge. My mom, who lost her own mother when she was young, came from a big family. She had lots of cousins, and lots of positive relationship role models, which I'd witness at holidays and the occasional family party. It was a different story within the four walls of my childhood home.

My father figure came more in the form of my grandfathers, both of whom I was very close with. My maternal grandfather, my Poppy, was a beautiful presence in my life. I can still hear him calling for me, a twinkle in his eye, "Where's my doll face?"

I also have vivid memories of my paternal grandfather—my Pa —sitting on his lap, twirling his chest hairs, asking him if he was scared of dying. He was always so calm, and he loved to share tales of Pearl Harbor, his life, and the war.

Both Poppy and Pa filled my life with the warmth, love, and protection I craved. Both passed when I was eighteen years old, on December 27th and August 27th. In a matter of eight months, POOF! That love was gone. At that point, I became the man in my own life.

Growing up, there was no trace of a romantic, healthy relationship in my home. I can't recall my parents ever kissing or saying, "I love you," to each other. It was a toxic, nasty environment, filled with fighting and verbal abuse. My dad worked nights as an NYPD detective in Brooklyn—a tough job that he could never fully leave behind. I can still hear him shouting for me in that clipped, stern voice that made me wonder what I'd be getting in trouble for this time.

"Elizabeth! Come into the room! I have to talk to you!"

I'd panic, a million thoughts racing through my head.

Shit, what did I do? Did he find my pot?

It was an unnecessary interrogation, just to say, "Your mother and I are going out this evening." Conversations with my father might as well have taken place in a holding cell. The absence of affection was palpable.

When Dad came home from work, he would drink away the horrors he witnessed on the job. The anger he harbored flooded our house. He'd be drunk, arguing with my mother, and suddenly I'd hear tables flipping and items crashing down. Something in me knew, even at that young age, that it was my responsibility to be the protector of the house. And of her.

One night, when I was eight, my mom and I heard *Pop! Pop! Pop!* in the kitchen. It sounded like gunshots. My dad wasn't home, and I remember being so scared as my mom sent me off to investigate, not knowing what I would be walking into. It turned out to be hard-boiled eggs, jumping out of the pot and hitting the floor.

Years later, when I was sixteen, I was getting ready to go to a party. Robe on, towel wrapped around my head, I walked into another room to find my dad on his knees with a gun in his mouth. I knelt down in front of him, staring down the barrel of the gun, and pleaded with him. He acquiesced. A few hours later, at a hotel with some friends, I found myself replaying the scene that I'd just witnessed, silently reliving the fact that I'd just coaxed my father out of ending his life.

My first car? My mom went with me. I ended up with a Mitsubishi Eclipse, a real piece of shit lemon that didn't even have a stereo system. I put a boombox in the back! My dad should have been there to help me negotiate.

My dance recitals growing up? My dad should have been there to cheer me on. If I needed five dollars? It was always a song and dance. I started working at eleven years old, just to prove I could take care of myself and wouldn't play into his rules. He always did what he wanted to do, what he needed to do, while I ached for the love and protection that a father typically provides.

Yes, that made me tough. It also left a huge void that lingers to this day. To be the sole provider for myself and my daughter, being completely on my own when it comes to major life decisions and roadblocks—like recently when I needed a co-signer to buy a house—makes me incredibly resentful towards him. There was never a feeling of, *I'll be okay—my dad will take care of it.*

It was no surprise that aversion towards control and authority bled into my love life. Romantically, I'd wander in and out of very shallow relationships, then sneaking off in the middle of the night.

I took on the stereotypically masculine role—no attachment, no commitment. The second anything resembled either of those things, I would feel like a noose was tightening around my neck. I couldn't breathe. I needed out.

I don't want a man. I'm gonna adopt a baby at thirty and be a successful businesswoman.

The yearning to escape didn't just apply to dating. I longed to be *free*. Countless times as a child and teen, I packed up black garbage bags full of my things and 'ran away.' I couldn't wait to get off of Long Island, to travel and see the world—to be on stage—to be a star—performing in any capacity as a dancer, actor, and model served as an escape. Those worlds of make-believe were my ticket out, and so I put everything I had into making that dream happen. It was one of the only aspects of my younger years that truly made me happy.

So, I made it happen. After high school, I was free as a bird. Got out of Dodge. Stayed single, traveled, and lived my life to the fullest as I'd always imagined. I started checking off my bucket list and finding my stride as a performer.

My dad showed his love the best way he knew how and could,

by being a provider and protecting me when he was present. As he softens in his later years, I can see his pain, his tears. his love—and I pray God sends him forgiveness within himself to find peace and happiness. I love my father and want nothing more than for him to release his pain and know we all love him.

I just bought a little beach bungalow as I finished writing this book—and my dad helped me.

Then I met Mark.

As I approached a honky-tonk in Nashville the bright shining lights beamed a contrast to the darkness inside. As the door swung open and stepped foot inside, the looks and stares on the faces stopped me in my tracks. I assessed the environment before continuing to walk forward. The place was very dark, I could feel the heaviness.

Someone approached me and said, "You are such a bright light, Honey. When you walk through those doors this bright shining light is around you and you know when you walk in."

I guess the light does really shine through the darkness.

Later I got to see how dark that place could be and how it became the Devils Tavern.

2
MARK

I met my ex-husband when I was twenty-three years old. For the most part, it was a healthy, beautiful relationship that lasted seven years, three of which we were married. Mark was a man who looked great on paper. He owned a home with his brother. He had his own business. I remember the first time I met him, he was wearing a really nice watch.

He was big, strong, and oozed the energy of a man who really had his shit together—a true gentleman. He grew up in the next town over, and we met through mutual friends.

Mark was fit, muscular, and covered in tattoos, with dark hair and hazel eyes. You'd think a guy who came across as the total package was a shoo-in for a smoking hot sex life. The first time he met my family, I warned them not to be put off by his appearance. In reality, Mark was the opposite of the bad boy. I loved him, and he was a good man. But I didn't feel alive with him. I never wanted to make love with him. And for that reason, I truly believed there was something wrong with me.

That's not to say we didn't have a great run while it lasted. My life changed by leaps and bounds during those seven years we were together, professionally and emotionally. Unlike my subsequent relationships, Mark and I hardly fought. It was a peaceful period for me to grow, learn, and change.

From a psychological perspective, any therapist would tell you that Mark stepped in and took over my mom's role as the parental figure. He was the opposite of my father. After him, I went for men like my father. So, the first time, I thought I did it right. Mark coddled me and took care of me. Mark knew. "Your father fucked you up," he once said to me, "and I took over your mom's role."

Once we went shopping at a really expensive clothing store. We were only meant to stop in for a return, but he saw me looking around and said, "Hey, why don't you pick something out for yourself?"

I politely declined at first. Mind you, I never, ever had someone offer to buy me things, let alone take me shopping. Everything I had, I bought myself.

"Just take a look," he nudged. So, I did. I picked out a few dresses and slipped into the fitting room to try them on. I loved them all. "Get them all," he insisted.

I felt like Julia Roberts in Pretty Woman (minus the whole hooker bit). Yet, as glamorous as it was, I was still incredibly uncomfortable.

My brother Tom said it best when, years after my divorce, he observed, "Mark was your escape." We met on New Year's Eve, started dating in January, and I'd basically moved into his house by February. It all happened so fast. But Tom was right. Mark got me out of my house and onto the path of starting a new life.

He was so good to me during a period of my life in which, if I'm honest, I was probably at my worst. I was spoiled, although not necessarily in a financial sense. I was still working, hustling, and pursuing my dreams. I never lost my independence or my drive, no matter what relationship I was in. But having someone to come home to, someone who took care of me and comforted me ... I think I took a lot of that for granted. I never took the initiative to do household chores, like cleaning or vacuuming. I hated doing laundry. Mark always did it. I worked late hours at the studio, so as he was coming home I was heading out. We rarely ate dinner together, and I was certainly not up in the morning packing his lunches.

Thank God that's not the person I am today.

The other major thing that happened during my relationship with Mark was the rise of my life as a businesswoman. One Saturday, while Mark and I were at the gym, the manager approached me. He asked, "What do you do?"

"I'm a dancer," I replied, "And I also teach." I'd started dancing at the age of two—ballet, tap, jazz, hip hop—and then I went on to take ballroom and Latin lessons, eventually competing in both. In every studio I went to, I started as a student and ended up becoming an instructor.

"Well, why don't you do that here? Turn it into a fitness class."

This was before the days of Zumba and other trademarked, dance-based fitness workouts, and to be honest, I didn't really know what I was doing.

"You'll figure it out," he reassured me.

He was right; I did. I combined my Latin and hip-hop experience, sped up the music on my CDs, and just went for it. In the beginning, I only had three students, one who would later go on to become one of my best friends. In just a few weeks, the class began to grow. They asked if I would teach multiple classes. Soon after, I was teaching at several locations.

I'm pretty good at this! I remember thinking. But I still had the urge to perform, to be an actress. I saw teaching as a side hustle, something temporary to help pay the bills. I was so convinced it was just a placeholder that when Zumba came out and they asked me to get certified, I refused. Little did I realize that teaching these classes would eventually become the foundation for Wild Cherryz, a burlesque company that was my first business.

To this day, I stand firm that I never looked to make a career out of the industry. Instead, fitness found me.

Things were going well. My relationship was steady; I was teaching, auditioning, and chasing my dreams. All that came crashing down in 2008, when I fell prey to a major scam agency for actors that left me bankrupt and $250,000 in debt.

Up front, the company seemed perfectly legit. The auditions were normal, the offices were located in the Empire State Building, and there were very credible people and celebrities attached to the agency. The other actors and I had no reason to suspect anything at first. But as time went on, things started to feel off. They had us selling candy bars and various other weird gimmicks that didn't add up. The work wasn't consistent. So, I got out of there. I had no clue it was too late.

Soon after, I started receiving calls from multiple credit card companies. I owed a total of $250,000! Apparently, when we were hired, they used our social security number to open credit cards online in our names and had the bills sent to their office in the Empire State Building. They paid the minimum. Then they closed up shop, abandoned the office and the company, and stopped paying the bills. At that point, I got a phone call.

Lawyers were involved. The FBI was involved. "How did you not know?" they demanded, adding to my embarrassment and shame. There was nothing to be done. I went from having perfect credit to having to file for bankruptcy.

And this, my friends, is when I discovered what anxiety was. It first manifested in my body as a weird instinct that something was off. I remember exiting the subway and getting lightheaded as I walked the streets of New York, feeling like I was about to hit the pavement. At first, I thought it was my blood sugar because I had no other conditions that could cause such an intense physical response. My body knew, even before my brain did, that something wasn't right.

I was losing weight. I was stressed. My doctor tested me for everything. She finally sat me down and said, "Elizabeth, you have anxiety and panic attacks. Finish things up with the lawyer and this case, but understand this is a part of life. There will always be stress, and you're going to have to learn how to manage it."

Tail between my legs and broke, with my credit score destroyed, I shuffled back to Mark and to the gym and pleaded for my job back. I had quit everything to pursue acting. It was time to rebuild.

In the aftermath, the idea for Wild Cherryz was born. I can remember the exact moment, on the elliptical machine at the gym, staring outside, randomly thinking about Vegas, when the inspiration struck. I didn't want to audition anymore. I didn't want my fate to be in someone else's hand. At this point, I trusted no one. I'm starting my own damn company! I decided.

Wild Cherryz, my burlesque company, was a hybrid of studio classes and performances. We went on America's Got Talent. We performed all over New York State. I directed an off-Broadway show at The Cutting Room. We had so much fun, and I'm still friends with the girls from that company today. In addition to performing, I opened the Wild Cherryz Dance Studio in my hometown of East Meadow, New York.

It was a wonderful experience that rose out of a true crisis and lasted all through my marriage to Mark. But a few years in, I realized I really missed acting. So I got back on the horse, put myself out there, and started making some serious strides in my career. I was booking movies, I was filming, I was running my business...I was killing it, to be honest. Eventually I started to get restless with the studio. At nearly thirty-one years old, I'd spent my whole life trying to get away from my hometown, and there I was commuting back and forth from Queens to East Meadow on a daily basis. But I had built a huge clientele and didn't want to throw away all the success it had generated. So, I passed it on to one of my instructors, with an agreement to continue teaching while wiping my hands clean of the business side. I turned my focus to my life and career in New York City.

The transition would have gone smoothly had I not also been

restless in my marriage. Mark and I filed for divorce in July, and the change of hands for the studio happened August 31st. It was like pulling at one loose string and watching the whole blanket I'd knitted unravel.

My marriage with Mark ended for many reasons, the biggest one being I simply wasn't the wife he needed me to be. If I'm honest, I knew it from the day I walked down the aisle. As that line to him grew shorter and shorter, I suddenly couldn't breathe. I had no saliva in my mouth. My dad looked at me and said, "You do not have to do this. We can get in the car and go."

How could I do that to Mark? I thought. How do I leave him up there? Something in me couldn't leave him hanging. As I continued down the aisle, I was so nervous. It was like I wasn't even there.

I had too many dreams to chase and passions to fulfill. I still wanted to travel, be free, and live life on my terms. I wasn't ready for Mark, and I definitely wasn't ready to be a wife. We were ships in the night, existing together, passing through, but never truly connecting.

After my divorce I learned to never speak out of anger or to use my words to hurt someone because I am hurting. I swore to myself I would never be that person again. I understood more what a man needs and wants. I respected the man more. I had a better understanding of the feminine role in life—not so pro independence and I don't need a man's mentality.

Now, almost ten years later, I am ready.

3
DAVE

Life was a mess. I was divorcing the man I'd been with for seven years, I was living in a $2,500 per month apartment in Queens that I could not afford, and I was closing my studio, my first business, which meant I was about to be unemployed.

All I had left were my dogs. My babies. Those dogs went through everything with me. I was in a SERIOUS funk.

Driving up to our annual family trip to "The Ranch," which is near Lake George, I remember gunning the gas, full speed ahead, just me and the dogs. I was so relieved to be there and away from everything, but I was really out of it. Right after I arrived, my brother Tom walked into my room, stared at me, and said, "Liz, you bought cat food."

"What?!" I could have sworn it was a wolf on the bag. It was not. It was a friggin' bobcat. That's how much I was not present.

Weight fell off me as I gained anxiety by the minute. This

time, the anxiety felt like an old friend. I knew what it was, and I was comfortable just sitting in its silence, on my own, as ending after ending unfolded. Suddenly out of nowhere, there was Dave.

I'd met Dave the year prior while I was still married to Mark. When we saw each other again at The Ranch he invited me out for a ride on his motorcycle. I was in full-on divorce fatigue and not in the head space for dating. Dave was not my type at all. He was tall and thin. Not muscular. Blonde hair, blue eyes. Not into fitness. No tattoos. I continued to decline his invitations, but he was persistent.

In the meantime, my friend Warren, another motorcycle enthusiast, took me on a ride. Warren was safe company. I knew he didn't have any agenda other than to show me the freedom of the open road.

That day out on the motorcycle with Warren jolted me into the present moment. The smell of the Adirondack Mountains. The feel of the cold, crisp air whipping against my skin. The pure, unspoiled beauty of nature surrounding me.

I snapped out of it. I thought, What the fuck am I doing? I can't give up now! My dogs need me!

After that ride, a new vision for my life started to come

together. I would find a roommate to help with the rent. I would teach. I would bartend. I would do whatever it took to get back into the game. I fell in love with motorcycles that day, and I never looked back.

Dave was persistent. For someone who appeared super clean-cut on the outside, he had a serious bad boy lurking underneath. The next time I ran into him, fresh off my bike high from my ride with Warren, I boldly said, "Hey, let's go for a ride. I'm ready."

That trip to The Ranch saved my life in so many ways.

I was with Dave for three pretty wonderful years. We went back and forth for a year—he came to Queens; I went to Jersey. I ended up falling in love with the countryside. My dogs loved having a yard to run in. Being in nature felt peaceful and healing. The most life-changing thing about my relationship with Dave, though, was the intimacy. It ignited me.

I had been with the same guy for seven years and I didn't know anything else, and suddenly I felt like a goddess. The first time Dave went down on me, it hit me—Ooh, he is a bad boy. I loved sex! How did I go through life for this long without realizing the pleasure I'd been missing out on? Without orgasms! As a burlesque performer,

The Light in the Devil's Tavern

I spent most of my twenties presenting myself as sexy and flirtatious, but never really engaging past that. It was a character I played, part of the gig. At almost thirty-one, and for the first time in my life, I was truly connecting with my sensuality and sexuality.

As things with Dave progressed, both in and out of the bedroom, I hustled at work. I bartended, Wednesday nights and Sundays and taught twenty-five fitness classes a week all over New York. At this point, I had to give up acting. My knees were shot. I could barely walk up the stairs. I couldn't afford coaches, and I couldn't afford to take the time off from work to go on auditions. I needed to survive.

It'll be there later in life, I told myself. I can always play a grandmother.

In the meantime, I stayed close to Warren, who continued taking me on rides, fueling my love for motorcycles even more. I even flew out to New Mexico for a two week ride to Sturgis Motorcycle Rally for the sixty-fifth anniversary. It was one of the most amazing experiences of my life.

Although things were falling back into place, something was still amiss. That passion that drove me to create Wild Cherryz, to take control of my life and my destiny, was calling to me once again. It wasn't enough to just survive. It was time to thrive.

Despite growing up on Long Island and choreographing and performing throughout New York, I was a country girl at heart. When I was at The Ranch, or out in nature, surrounded by horses, cowboys, and music, I felt most at home. As this realization hit me, country music was starting to rise in popularity, becoming more mainstream. I even snuck in a Jason Aldean/Luke Bryan song on one of my playlists for my fitness classes in Queens.

One day at the gym, I looked out the window at the Manhattan skyline and lightning struck once again.

That's it! I thought. There are no country fitness programs out there.

I called it "Country Fit" at first, but someone had already been using that name. Instead, I came up with "Country Fusion" because it's fused with wild cards from my non-country background—salsa, cha cha, hip hop, bachata, swing dance, and more. Soon after the idea sparked, I hopped on the motorcycle, and as I rode, the details of the program instantly fell into place. After years in the fitness industry, I knew exactly what I wanted the format to be: fifty-minute classes based on LIIT (Low Intensity Interval Training) derived from a music playlist of fifteen songs, with four of them being wild cards.

As Country Fusion came together, I was also in the process of moving to New Jersey with Dave. The transition was tough, because even though I loved it out in nature and I loved Dave, I was making really good money in New York. Starting from scratch out there meant building new relationships and contacts, and taking a serious pay cut as a result. I just have to bite the bullet and rebuild, I thought to myself.

And that's what I did. I commuted to New York for the odd job here and there because I still needed that Manhattan money. Once I got things going in Jersey, I rented out space in two different locations to start teaching Country Fusion. I created a Groupon and gave incentives for my ladies from other classes to come try it out. Country Fusion rose from a spark of an idea to two hundred clients in that first go.

While Wild Cherryz played to my artistic side, with designing costumes, dancing, and acting, Country Fusion was a total lifestyle endeavor. It was a fitness program accessible to everyone, and it still continues to grow and evolve. The empowerment I felt in building businesses directly correlated with the type of men I attracted…and not in a good way. This rise of my success consistently coincided with the demise of my relationships.

"Women can have it all!" Or so we've been promised. But can we really?

After my divorce, my patterns with men changed. I started exclusively dating men like my father. For example, with Dave, there was an element of control that I needed to rebel against. He was selfish and very much set in his ways. His defense? "I have to be hard on you and not give you what you want so history doesn't repeat itself." He was referring to my divorce. Everything hinged on his wants and his needs, from moving to New Jersey because that's where he wanted to live, to where we vacationed and spent our free time—all things I wanted to share with him. He never went on any of my family trips, and refused to participate in our annual Christmas tradition of seeing the Rockefeller tree and St. Patrick's Cathedral, followed by dinner in Little Italy.

I'm much more of a free spirit, so there was only so much I could take without completely losing myself once again. Leaving

The Light in the Devil's Tavern

Dave was hard because I loved him. I gave up everything to be with him. I was addicted to the euphoria of it all. I needed it in my life. Dave wanted to get married and have children, but on his timeline. Dirt bikes, and motorcycles, and his mother all took priority. He wasn't ready. In the end, what finally broke us was that I was. I wanted a baby. And I was tired of being so far down the timeline.

I learned that someone may love you and you may love them but if we are not healed and don't know our traumas and triggers yet, a relationship will most likely not work.

"I love you," I said to him. "But I love myself more."

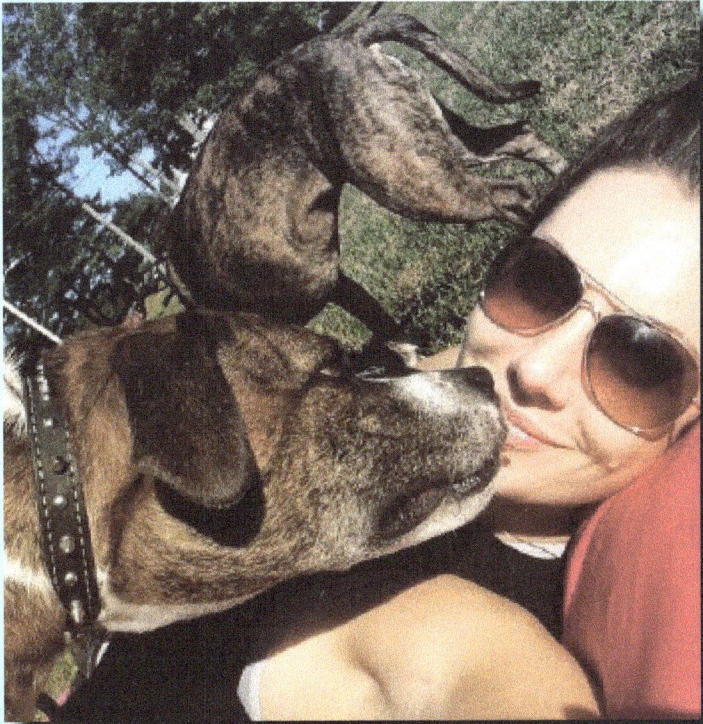

4
ADAM

"Look at you, of course I wanted to have a baby with you."

"There's two cars, my ex is ready to ride. You still need some work to ride."

"Thought you were going to get fat when you got pregnant."

"I can't wait to see you give birth and shit yourself."

It was an absolute nightmare. He was an absolute nightmare. And there I was, pregnant with his child.

Adam and I were dance partners, and the sparks that flew the first time we danced together were fire. He was six years younger than me, tall, with dark hair and crystal blue eyes. They were such a distinctive blue that while I was pregnant, I prayed to God that the baby didn't get his eyes. He wasn't necessarily the best-looking guy, but he had unique features that caught my eye, like the way his upper lip bulged out a bit.

He knew I'd left Dave because I wanted to have kids. The

good parts were so incredibly good. That euphoric feeling I first experienced with Dave was back and better than ever. And that's what you want to remember, right? The memories make you feel good. Not the horrible demise of it all.

We both wanted a child, and, worst-case scenario that we didn't work out, we'd just figure out a way to co-parent. Sounds practical in theory, but I realized after it was too late how little I actually knew this man. The fact that we both wanted a child was fine, but for Adam, having a baby together was a means to gain access and control over me.

After I got pregnant, Adam decided he wanted to move to Arizona, where he had lived briefly before I met him in New Jersey. He kept saying that for us to be a family we should be alone and away from everyone. It didn't make a lot of sense to me, but I agreed to take a trip out to Arizona to take a look around. I'll admit, it was gorgeous.

"I love it here," I told him. "But I'm not going to move here. Maybe when the baby's two or three, but not now."

My doctor was back in Jersey. Our families were there. Our baby would be the first grandchild, and I didn't want to move across the country, away from everyone in our support system. Adam was enraged that I wouldn't go.

After that discussion, I knew something was off. We had the convo on a Tuesday, and we had a doctor's appointment the following Monday. At this point it's clearly not working out and I've confirmed I'm not moving to Arizona. That Thursday, I called Adam to confirm that he'd be at the appointment and I could hear that he was in the car.

"Where are you?" I asked, concerned. He said he was heading to Upstate New York. Now I was getting suspicious.

Again I asked, "Are you going to be there Monday?" That's all I cared about. It was the first big doctor's appointment, where we would learn if we were having a boy or a girl.

Sunday night rolled around and I got a call from him. He was at the airport, trying to make his way back. Though he did make it home on Sunday, he still wasn't able to make the appointment because of work. He asked, "Can we change it?"

I'd had enough. We'd had that appointment for months. If he hadn't taken off work on Thursday and Friday, he wouldn't have had a schedule conflict with work on Monday. With tears in my eyes, I made the decision that it was the last time I was going to let him hurt me. As it turns out, he had actually gone down to Georgia (where his ex lived) because he was planning on moving there, and that trip had been to start setting things in motion. I remember calling Dave and begging him to come with me to the appointment. I really wanted to have a man with me.

"This is really hard for me, Liz," he told me. It was. But I was desperate to have a man by my side for that moment. Dave showed up. The man with whom I'd broken up because he didn't want to have children ended up being the one in the room the day I learned I was having a baby girl.

Adam called relentlessly that day, fuming over the fact that Dave went to the appointment with me. I repeatedly denied his phone calls.

"Listen, cowboy, your rodeo's over," I told him.

After that, more and more lies started to explode like tiny little bombs in the midst of a vast, convoluted minefield. At first, his ex was back in the picture. Then she wasn't. His sister got involved, exposing more of his sordid past. Eventually, I tracked down his mother at work, demanding to know what was going on. Some of the history she revealed about Adam was frightening, including his inability to show emotion from a very young age. All of this I learned while five months pregnant with his child.

Adam was one of those guys whom none of my friends or family really liked. There was something about him; it was in the eyes. When I first got pregnant, we were sitting next to each other on the couch and I remember looking at him and just saying, "You're not capable of loving."

Taken aback, he retorted, "What do you mean?"

"I don't know." I didn't know exactly how to put my finger on it. "You feel empty," I said. "I can't latch onto anything." I wanted to love him, but I couldn't. "You don't love yourself."

When I was five-and-a-half months pregnant with our daughter, Adam left for good. He packed up a backpack and headed out of town. He told me I lit "grenades" in his life, but the reality was, I simply exposed him for the liar, gaslighter, and manipulator he truly was.

In his dramatic exit, he continued to call me to warn me that he was changing his phone number. He wanted me to know exactly where he was going and what he was doing as he was simultaneously threatening to cut me off forever. It was almost like reverse stalking, where instead of him tracking and following me, he continued to make sure I knew where he was at all times. At one point he came groveling back, claiming he did want us to be a family, but I was having none of it. He'd exposed himself for who he truly was and I could never look past that.

The drama didn't end there, however. Does it ever end with a narcissist? Shortly after he left, I was at a wedding in Lake George when I received a Facebook message from Adam's ex-girlfriend Eva. She was nosing around about my pregnancy, and it was clear she wanted more information. I quickly shut it down, telling her I didn't want any part of it. She needed to keep him down there, and keep him away from me.

Next thing I knew, I got a phone call from Eva with Adam in the background. They were fighting, with a gun involved. It was total chaos.

Then Abby, another ex from Arizona, came out of the woodwork. She was also still involved with him, and he was playing her too. Now I was almost six months pregnant, dealing with this shit show. His schemes continued, from trying to convince Eva that they should take me to court to get full custody of the baby, to threatening me that he wouldn't pay any child-support at all.

The stories that came out about Adam during this time were bone-chilling. Eva revealed that he had once killed two kittens with his bare hands, and had lit a bar on fire in Arizona. She told me that one time they were in the car, fighting, and she begged him to tell her where they were going. As they drove, the coldness she saw in his eyes was enough to make her physically jump out of a moving car to get away from him. Abby had similar stories, including one time he set her clothes on fire.

At one point, after digesting all this information, I felt sick knowing I was carrying his baby. That feeling only lasted about twenty-four hours. I remember crying with my mom and deciding,

"No. This baby is mine."

I made the choice to change my mindset, filtering out the stories about this monster and focusing on the human growing inside me.

In hindsight, the writing was on the wall with Adam. I got a teaser of his sociopathic tendencies during our trip to Arizona when I was pregnant. But without the validation of the other women and exes in his life, I couldn't see him for who he truly was. It didn't feel real.

One night during that trip, while he was trying to sell me the whole "We'll have a nice life in Arizona," thing, I spoke with one of his friend's wives whose brother was about to become a cop.

"My dad's a cop!" I started to share with her.

Before I could continue, Adam, who was not part of the conversation, cut in with, "Yeah, Liz is a little shit cop kid." I was dumbfounded. I remember excusing myself to go to the bathroom, attempting to calm myself down as my pregnancy hormones raged.

I can't stand this motherfucker.

When I returned to the table he put his arm around me, and I snaked out of it.

"I told him he can't talk to you like that," his friend's wife confided.

My instant reaction was, "He's not going to listen to you."

I don't know if it was the hormones or what, but in that moment I came very close to snapping from the stress. The knife on the table caught my eye, its shiny, sharp edge tempting me to stab him in the leg. Instead, I asked for a glass of water, figuring I'd throw it at him on our way out. The security guy stopped me. "I'm sorry Ma'am, but you can't leave with the glass."

Adam obnoxiously taunted me. "Yeah Liz, this isn't New York. You can't just do whatever you want."

That was it. I took a swing at him, right there, five months pregnant in the dirt parking lot. That fucker moved fast, so I missed him. We got in the car and I started to cry. I was driving, and I remember stopping short and trying to kick him out. I wanted to leave his ass in the desert.

When I was eight months pregnant, I decided to name the baby Danika. On the way to my baby shower, I googled what it meant: "morning star," in Slavic. I looked at the coinciding image, thinking I would get it as a tattoo, only to find Lucifer staring back at me. The story goes that initially, Lucifer was the Angel of Light and Good. He was the "morning star" until his ego got the best of him, and he died and became the Devil.

Sounds familiar. What the hell, Liz? You're probably thinking. Why the fuck did you even speak to this guy after that? Did you really need confirmation from those other women to know he was an asshole?

The Light in the Devil's Tavern

Maybe I did. When you're involved with someone who has sociopathic tendencies, it's not unusual to feel crazy at times. That's part of the manipulation. The hot and cold, the back and forth, the charmer to the devil. It's enough to make your head spin. Add a healthy dose of pregnancy hormones on top, and most days, you don't know what you should be thinking or feeling. By the time Adam left (and I made it clear he was not to come back) the only thing that mattered to me was delivering a healthy baby.

So that's what I focused on. I spent the rest of my pregnancy surrounded by friends and family. I worked and danced right up to my due date. I dated! Most of the time it was just one date (hey, a girl's gotta eat!), but if it went past that I always disclosed the pregnancy. At the time I wasn't necessarily looking for romance. Being a woman and pregnant, not having someone to rub and kiss your belly, or even just wake up to...there was a void. It was just me working all the time. I had my two dogs and my condo, but I was on my own. On the positive side, I had an amazing support system in my family and friends. They threw me two huge baby showers. The women that religiously took my classes became my friends and my protectors. Even the guys I went on dates with were all really supportive, offering to look after things around the house and shovel snow in the winter. They were really kind.

I should also mention that even though I lost my head in my relationship, my business brain remained fully intact. As Country Fusion and my presence in the fitness industry grew, I was contacted by the founder of SCW Fitness. She was one of my earliest champions whom I met on my dance and fitness journey, and I have only the greatest respect for her and what she's built. She really believed in me and Country Fusion, and wanted to help me expand. However, I was a little gun-shy about jumping right in after what had happened with the agency scam/bankruptcy in my twenties.

I said to myself, "I'll try going on a fitness tour in one city to get my brand out there and see what happens."

We started with Dallas, and as soon as I got there, I realized it was legit and a highly lucrative opportunity. I was in. Together, we revamped my whole business model, from my website to my logo. I incorporated tutorials, online workout videos, and online certifications so that I could now operate online and in person, which was key because of my pregnancy. I didn't know how my body would react to the pregnancy and how that would impact my teaching. Not to mention, years later when COVID hit, that online program was a business-saver. My studio was forced to close on a Monday, and by Tuesday I had Zoom classes going live. I didn't miss a beat.

My relationship with SCW lasted for years. I toured all over the country and the world—New York, San Francisco, Dallas, Orlando, DC, Chicago, and Canada, to name a few. In each city I certified instructors, studios and gyms in the Country Fusion brand.

It's puzzling, to no one more than me, how I could build this fitness empire and achieve so many of my goals and dreams, and yet have the worst luck and instincts when it came to men. I wish I could tell you that was the end of Adam, but true to form, he has popped in and out of my life story continuously for the past six years. Are you ever really rid of a man, once you have a child with him?

When Danika was born, I did not list his name on the birth certificate. He didn't deserve it. He missed most of my pregnancy, every doctor's appointment, and even her birth. He showed up for her birthday one time (her first) and that was it. As far as I'm concerned, all Danika needs to know is, "My dad is Adam and he lives in Arizona."

I saw what an awful human being looks like. What a bad and toxic person looks like. The first time I danced with the devil. What a person with darkness in their eyes and an empty soul feels like. Naïve to it cause it was my first encounter. There are people who will use you, hurt you, abandon you, and feel nothing cause they have created a story to their actions. I saw a glimpse of his heart when he first came back and cried then poof it goes away once the ego comes back. I learned how strong I was in this relationship. How far I will go to protect myself and my unborn child.

I wish I could tell you that I learned my lesson after dating him, but if I had, this book probably wouldn't exist. My journey with business and my journey with men ran along two parallel, non-intersecting roads. With the men, I sped down the highway of emotional abuse and destruction, slamming into potholes, taking wrong turns at every intersection.

Next up on the ride is Andrew.

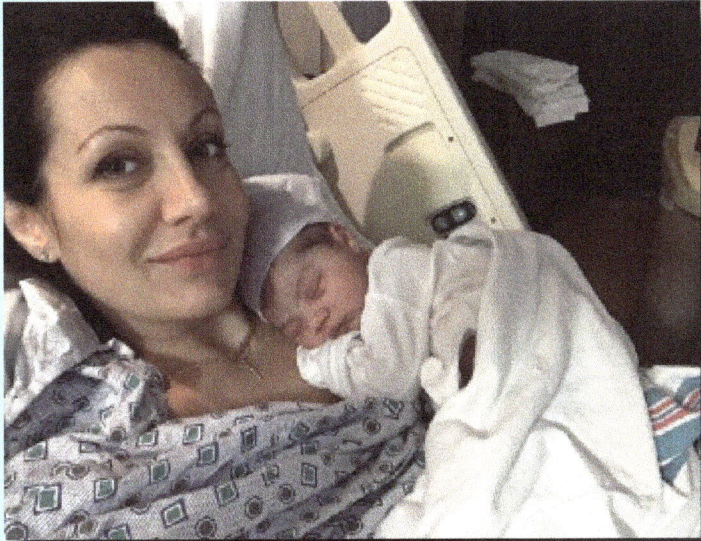

5
ANDREW

We've reached the part of the fairytale where Danika is four months old, I'm a single mom living alone in New Jersey, and all I wanted was a steak dinner. It was my first real night out since having the baby, so my friend and I headed to the restaurant to cash in on that craving. After dinner, while sitting at the table drinking the last of my glass of wine, he walked in.

The second I laid eyes on Andrew, I was struck with a feeling that I knew him. Memories flashed through my head as I tried to place him, but I came up with nothing. We continued staring at each other until I finally broke the ice and walked up to him.

"Do I know you?" I asked.

We started dating pretty much immediately. My connection with Andrew was one of the most crazy, intense experiences of my life. When we were together and our bodies were skin to skin, I could feel his energy. There was a darkness roaring and swirling inside his body, drawing me in. Andrew had a traumatic past, filled with sexual abuse and fighting, and I could see that little boy inside of him. He called to me, like a cry for help, wondering if it was safe to come out. I can remember a moment of him lying on top of me and I could feel that darkness. It was a spiritual connection that sounds mad to explain, but was also raw and real: I felt and saw his soul.

I think, particularly as women, when we are in a vulnerable place we can often mistake that connection for a sign that we've found our soulmate. Those unexplainable energies are all too often the reason we stay far longer in a relationship than we're meant to. When I met Andrew, it was easy to overlook a lot of the warning signs, because it felt like something bigger than both of us drew us together. I was a newly single mother, craving a man and a father for my daughter. And Andrew...well, Andrew was incredibly handsome. Perfect nose structure, tall, muscular, tattoo-covered, and a great face. But most of all, Andrew was fun. After all I'd gone through with Adam and my pregnancy and being out on my own, I needed that. Together we were two free spirits. He was the Bonnie to my Clyde. And though he wasn't packing all that much down there, it was still very, very intimate.

But Andrew was another textbook narcissist. He was toxic in a way that was different from Adam. While Adam had a soulless, inflated sense of self, Andrew's toxicity fell under the self-loathing department.

"I don't deserve you," he would say. "You can do better." Yet no matter how many times I tried to break things off, he wouldn't let me move on.

As Andrew's true colors revealed themselves, I knew I had to get out. I remember driving to Indiana for a performance, and on my way there I just kept praying to God to sever the soul ties between us.

"Whatever this is, please end it. This is no good for me. I don't want this."

When I got home from the trip, he immediately wanted to see me and made up excuses to come by. He claimed he needed to pick up something from my house, and then stole my underwear. I had to change my phone number. I got out of my car lease nine months early to get a new, unrecognizable car, and moved in with my Grandma Ronnie so Andrew couldn't track me down. He started showing up at my work. He refused to let me go.

Andrew also had loads of toxic relationships surrounding him. There was his ex-girlfriend in the background (not completely new territory for me) who was a bit crazy and claimed he could date anyone else but me. They had this toxic dance going, where he would run from her to me, making her a constant, irritating presence.

Immediately after we broke up, he started dating someone new, married her, and knocked her up in record time. Yet throughout that relationship, he still continued to contact me. He wanted to adopt Danika. He needed to see me.

At this point, it was 2020 and the pandemic was in full swing. Andrew contacted me once more, insisting on meeting me for God knows what reason. I foolishly thought that telling him Danika and I had COVID would put him off. Instead, in a CVS parking lot, I found myself face to face with a man begging for me to kiss him and give him COVID as retribution for what he'd done.

Looking back, I realize the toxicity with these men felt comfortable because it was a reflection of the dynamics in my childhood home. It was where I felt like I belonged. I had no interest in the high-value man…he was too straight, too normal. I preferred "unknown" territory.

Danika growing up with a father was important to me, particularly back then. I know subconsciously I accelerated the whole dating experience while she was a baby so she'd never experience the void.

I never wanted to have the conversation, "Momma, who is my dad?" Despite growing up in a household that wasn't exactly the prototype for a happy, functional family, I still had a father. I was surrounded by that male presence. I wanted that for my daughter. And perhaps, with such a clear mission in place, I became blinded to the fact that having no father was better, safer, and healthier for my child than the toxic dance I'd been performing for years with these men.

To this day, Andrew will still contact me from time to time. I choose not to engage. There is peace now. He brought me the greatest lessons. I saw darkness on a soul level with him, and I saw the other side. I was in the beginnings of finding my inner light and purpose.

I learned what crazy looks like. This was the most toxic, crazy, exhausting relationship. I look back and I don't know how I did that dance for as long as I did. I was not in the right mind set. Connection and wanting that family was in the forefront throwing logic out the window. That relationship taught me red flags, toxic patterns, and what not to do.

6
TIM

As life as a single mom continued, and Andrew and I engaged in our cat and mouse game, I also had Adam still circling, popping in and out at will.

Just like I knew I needed to get away from Long Island, I also knew instinctively that New Jersey wasn't my last stop. I settled there for awhile, however. Moving to Arizona with Adam wasn't the answer. I had Danika in New Jersey. I met Adam and Andrew in New Jersey. I taught burlesque, I performed and competed in Ballroom and Latin, and I built Country Fusion there. My career and reputation was building, and I was even credited for singlehandedly bringing country line dancing back to New Jersey. Clients and friends kept planting the seeds to take Country Fusion down to Nashville.

"You'll make a killing there," they told me. "There's nothing like it!"

Nashville had always called to me, so it was all very tempting. But if my main goal was to build a stable life for my daughter and to meet someone, it wasn't the time to pick up and start all over again.

Tim and I met right when COVID hit, and I remember thinking he had the most beautiful blue eyes I'd ever seen. Blond hair, muscular build, a beard ... he was a real tatted up, sexy biker guy. Simply put, he was hot, and definitely packing heat. Let me tell you, we had some great times. Since lockdown began shortly after we started dating, Tim and I had a lot of time alone together, just the two of us. I taught him to dance in my empty studio. We'd hop in his pickup truck and drive out to the country to gaze at the stars. We stayed in cabins in the woods, and rented an RV to drive down to Gatlinburg and the Shenandoah Valley. Even though the world was shut down, Tim and I made the open road our own little adventure.

Everything also moved really fast because of the pandemic. I got wrapped up very quickly in my world with Tim, happy to avoid any red flags. Less than a year into dating, we were already talking about buying a house together. Then COVID started to slow down and the world began opening back up.

I can pinpoint the exact moment it started to unravel, when we attended a motorcycle party out on Long Island. He slyly asked if I was "going to behave," a comment I found ironic given the type of party we were about to attend. What Tim didn't realize was that because he was taking me to a party on Long Island (where I grew up) I would end up knowing quite a few people there. While we were all holed up in our COVID bubble, Tim had me all to himself. Now he was seeing me out in the wild, working a room, chatting with the women and the wives and all the guys in his motorcycle club. He was not happy. A switch went off in him. That was when the power struggle began.

"You know Liz, not everyone gets to be with the alpha," he scoffed. "You're special, but I'm special too."

With that, he pretty much whipped out a portfolio of his past modeling pictures to prove to me how special he was. I remember saying to myself, "What the hell is going on? Who is this person?"

Just like with Adam, the second he felt threatened in any way, and was no longer the center of attention, he puffed his chest, peacocked his feathers, and did what he could to make me feel small.

Tim's ex-girlfriend was, unbeknownst to me, still in the background (here we go again!). She was my polar opposite—a quiet, tiny wallflower. While she was lurking around, he and I were frighteningly close to buying a house. Like, "We're going through the inspection" close. Once more my instincts kicked in, gnawing at me. I started to do some detective work, which I'd gotten pretty good at thanks to Adam and Andrew, and more importantly, I trusted my gut.

The second I discovered the ex, I was done. Done with men. Done with the drama. End of story. The shock of discovering once again there was someone else in the background hit me in my core.

I had to stop trying to force this cookie-cutter life and take a good, hard look at what was best for my and Danika's future. It was time to stop repeating history, and time to start rewriting it.

Signs and intuitions have always been powerful within me, particularly when it came to business. For example, the idea for Wild Cherryz was born on an elliptical machine. I looked out the window to the left and a vision came to me. That was it. That's what I had to do. The same thing happened with Country Fusion. I was teaching in Queens and again, I looked out the window to the left and saw the Manhattan skyline. A vision to create a country fitness program struck like lightning. Despite there being no other signs or guidance, I just went for it. The blinders came off and my vision was super clear.

After Tim, I had that same clarity. I started prepping the business to relocate headquarters. Country Fusion remained in New Jersey and was inherited by my trained Country Fusion instructors, essentially inciting the beginning of my franchise.

The next step was to actually go to Nashville and find a space. Downtown prices were ridiculously high, and a guy I met with suggested I check out Midtown. So, I did. As I stood outside a building in Midtown, I saw a security guy. First, he asked for my ID to get in. The guy next to him added, "Yeah, and your credit card too."

"Really?" I said. My New York sass was no match for these southerners. "Why don't you take my cash while you're at it?"

A smile spread across his face. "All right, come in. I like you. Let me buy you a drink."

"Oh, you're gonna take my cash and buy me a drink with it?" I bantered back. We ended up going in, and I explained what I was looking for. He suggested I check out a place called Nashville Palace, which I'd never heard of.

The next day we went there, and of course, it was closed due to COVID. We headed over to the gas station, and as I peered into the adjacent lot I saw a honky-tonk lit up, with a sign that said, "Music City Bar and Grill." Something told me not to leave just let. "We need to go there."

We went into the honky-tonk and started dancing. The bouncer introduced me to his "cousin" who told me about an entire strip mall right next door that would be a perfect spot for the studio. Once that ball was in motion, the rest of the move fell into place.

It's very easy to adopt the victim mentality of "Why does this keep happening to me?" When things fell apart with Tim, I had to do some serious soul-searching to figure out what the next phase of my life was going to look like.

I wanted to bring line dancing back to Nashville, where locals and tourists could come together and learn everything from two-step to country swing, to line dancing. to Country Fusion, and then take those skills out that night. I wanted to create a place that felt like home, so much so that our slogan is "Where sneakers and water bottles meet whiskey and cowboy boots."

Once I set up shop, I started working on Broadway and dancing at the honky-tonk at night. I danced and performed in the Country

Music Awards (CMAs), choreographed for various country artists, and even appeared in a few music videos on CMT. In less than two years, I moved to a new state, built a new everything, and achieved my goal of bringing dancing back to Nashville.

One of the greatest compliments I've ever received was being recognized for that by people who've lived in Music City their whole lives. The other greatest compliment? When tourists from various cities and countries come back for more. Not to mention, I was pretty much the first female in the game.

None of this would have happened if I had bought that house in New Jersey with Tim. Though the fallout and his behavior was so shitty, it was a blessing that it happened how and when it did. It was the push I needed to get back in the car and continue driving down I-80, just as I'd imagined years earlier when I ended my marriage and crossed state lines.

I had my daughter, my work, a growing reputation and a booming business.

Tim was a quick Covid relationship and that sealed the deal on not looking for that family and rushing into things. This ending pushed me to stop and look forward to my dreams and goals and let things unfold.

Damn it if I was gonna let a cowboy take any of that away from me! But boy, did Charlie try.

7
CHARLIE

She is a whiskey queen
A little dancin' hunny
A splash of class & sass
All mixed up in a vodka glass
A life that's young
And a soul that's old

Sometimes you chalk it up as a lesson learned
No matter how bad you get burned
Just one more fall from playing the part
But I'm tougher than the scars
That cover this heart

Doing good ain't going so great
Should have jumped off before they opened that gate
I really thought I could make it this time
I'll dust off these boots and get back in line

For One More Ride…..

It was April, 2021, and I was still doing the back and forth between Nashville and New Jersey, prepping for the move. One day, as my mom, my friend, Danika, and I were standing outside the honky-tonk chatting with the owner, I could feel someone behind me, staring. I looked over and sure enough, there was a tall guy, wearing a cowboy hat, staring. I returned to my conversation with the owner, but I could still feel his eyes on me. After a few glances back, I finally smiled. He smiled back.

My mom took Danika back to the hotel and I stayed at the bar to dance. It turned out he was performing there. His eyes stayed on me the entire night. At one point, as I was line dancing to Travis Tritt's "Bonnie and Clyde," he jumped off the stage with his guitar and started playing right alongside where I was dancing.

This guy's fun, I thought.

Later that night, as I sat at the bar nursing a drink, he swept on in.

"I've been watching you all night. I haven't kept my eyes off you. I always look at everyone to make sure they're having a good time, but I kept clocking where you were to make sure you didn't leave," he continued. "Even before you walked in, when you were outside standing there with your mom and your daughter. You looked like the cover model on a magazine. I just have to count the money real quick, but can I please buy you a drink? I'd love to talk to you, if that's okay. You captured my night."

Whoa, Dude. Intense.

There was something sweet about it though. So, I stayed. We talked. There was a spark, a connection. Charlie was a big guy, with arms that made you feel super safe and protected. He had broad shoulders, a huge chest, and a bit of a belly, probably due to all the smoking and drinking. Slightly less fit than I typically go for. But he had a really nice face, with dark hair and dark eyes. When he looked at me, it was like no one else existed.

The next day, I went back to dance and we hung out some more. He told me he had four kids, was divorced, but currently lived in North Carolina. He was doing the back and forth as well, with his plans to move in May and mine in June.

I went home to my mom that night and said, "I'm gonna marry that man. We have the most insane connection."

"I've never heard you say that," she responded. Because I hadn't. I didn't even know where it came from.

Charlie and I were both on the commuter track when it came to split lives and prepping to move, but we kept in touch regularly and talked constantly.

A few weeks in, the communication seemed to cool, and I didn't hear from him for a few days. Experience told me that was a red flag. I said to myself, "Your past has taught you that crazy as it may be, if you go to their Facebook profile and you see who's liking and commenting, you'll find your answer." I so deeply wished that wasn't true. But that's exactly how I found out he was engaged.

I messaged him.

You can pretty much tell me anything, I wrote, trying to squeeze the truth out. Just be open and be honest. I gave him an hour to respond. Then the bullshit started flowing in.

"It's not what you think, it's a promise ring," he pleaded. Whatever the fuck that is.

They've been on the outs.

He's focusing on his music.

He wanted to be friends with me while he was handling everything.

"You can go fuck yourself," I told him.

Charlie was another one that wouldn't take "no" for an answer. He tried to get booked to perform where I went line dancing in New Jersey. He texted me out of the blue, several times. Each message was laced with more and more excuses and promises that his engagement was really over. He was done for good. He was moving to Nashville. There was something about the situation that still pulled at my heart. The connection we had was real, and it was something I hadn't felt in a while. I was moving to a new city, where

The Light in the Devil's Tavern

I didn't know a ton of people. He could feel me caving. Before I could change my mind, he booked himself on a flight to New Jersey the weekend before I was due to move.

Red. Flag.

We did the on-again, off-again toxic dance for almost two years. Everyone knew that Charlie and I together were a mess. He was all over the place, his story constantly changing.

First, he claimed he was ready for a commitment because he knew that's what I wanted. But I wanted something solid, and Charlie could not get out of his own way.

"You're the prime rib and I'm the ballpark hot dog, " he would always say. He didn't feel he was good enough to be with me. He didn't have it. And while I did see the good in him, I didn't have it in me to fix another broken man. I needed to fix myself.

Aside from the drama with Charlie, I faced an unexpected amount of hate and adversity from the honky-tonk when I came to town. There was a lot of unfounded jealousy that ran so deep I actually questioned if I'd made the right move. As much as I loved country music, I was struggling deeply as a New Yorker in the South.

I was also in the midst of building the Country Fusion brand to reflect where I was at in life. The concept was my New York Burlesque days meets my new country honky-tonk life. I organized a photo shoot to launch this new chapter, and the man who ran the honky-tonk offered to let me use the space. I was very gracious about it, and planned to use the photos for upcoming promotions. As a nod to his generosity, I promised that when I posted the advertisements on social media I would tag him. That's what we always did in New York. It was an acknowledgment of gratitude, some free marketing, and nothing more.

The community went wild. Apparently tagging a married man in a picture from a professional photo shoot at his venue was a cardinal sin. I'm shocked they didn't try to drown me in holy water.

Instead, they took to the Internet. Hateful things were posted. One awful woman put up a picture of me, portraying me as some sort of she-devil. They were acting like I'd had an affair with the man instead of merely tagging him in a Facebook photo. I even tried to reason with some of the haters.

"Listen, I'm a brand. I'm a business. This is how I feed my daughter, and this has gotten out of hand." His wife refused to speak to me. The more I tried to defend myself, to stand up to the bullies, the more it got out of hand, eventually resulting in my getting banned from the honky-tonk.

Something good came out of it, though. One day, after picking Danika up from school, I put on a Netflix show. It was all about kids getting bullied in school. It hit me. There I was, a single mom in my late thirties, getting bullied by a bunch of grown-ups. They called me a "Yankee Whore"! Yes, they're the kind of people who still use the term Yankee. In response, since they took away my voice and my ability to connect with the community, I created a billboard for Country Fusion. And I put that fucking billboard right in front of the honky-tonk, where those bullies could see my face every day.

Once again, I didn't let that situation knock me down. I let it inspire me. I decided to create "Country Fusion for Kids," an anti-bullying movement where the instructors work with the children on self-empowerment, positivity, and words of affirmation. I wanted kids to walk away from the program feeling loved. Like they have a voice. Thinking about how many children take their own lives due to bullying broke my heart. After I came up with the idea for the program, I started implementing it in schools. Another business model that sprang out of the ashes of a low point in my life.

A few months later, I had to drop off a gift certificate at the honky-tonk—where I was still banned—and ran into Charlie. He was there with another woman, and honestly, it didn't bother me. We weren't together and he was free to do as he pleased. Two weeks after that, true to form, Charlie circled back one last time. It was just before Valentine's Day. He showed up at my studio, card in hand:

Liz, we've been through so much, and I've loved you through all of it. I'll be honored if you'd be my Valentine.

The card had choices:

YES

NO

HELL NO

HELL YEAH

We talked. He watched me dance. "I forgot how much I loved watching you dance," he told me. There was a depth to our connection. It wasn't just about the sex. It reminded me of what I'd had with Andrew.

"Liz you're not a girlfriend, you're a wife," he told me. "Our souls already knew one another. We just needed to get to know one another."

With that, he headed back to North Carolina, and I was back on the Liz/Charlie roller coaster. While he was gone that weekend, I noticed he shared something on Facebook that he didn't bother to tell me. Red flag. On Monday, I got a call.

"I can't do this. Not until I'm ready. Everything I've said and my feelings are true, but I'm not good enough for this."

It was dejá vu. I'd had almost the same conversation with Andrew a few years back. I said, "I know you're not, and I don't know why you keep coming back to me, trying before you're ready. I have to release you from my heart, and I have to move forward in my life without you."

The ride came to a screeching halt and I was at peace with it. So much so that two days later, I popped into the club where he was playing to wish him a happy fortieth birthday. Now remember, just a week or so prior he was at my studio professing his love. Wouldn't one assume there was no one else in the picture if he wanted me back so badly?

Wrong again. I walked in on his birthday and spotted the same woman he was with a few weeks before, standing at the back of the room while that son of a bitch was singing away on stage. I caught his eye and mouthed, "You fucking lying piece of shit."

"Oh shit," I saw him mutter.

I headed to the bathroom, and who did I hear from the stall? His girl, gushing to her friend about him. I couldn't help myself. I walked out and started chatting away. She had no idea who I was. She actually introduced herself as Charlie's girlfriend. They'd been dating since June. She was an emergency room nurse who lived in Virginia, and had driven out last minute for his birthday show.

It takes me a long time to get to the point of really being done and not just saying it, but when I get there, it's end game. I haven't talked to him since. I guess I needed that confirmation. I needed to accept him for who he truly was, and stop feeding into the fantasy that our connection and our love could somehow overcome his lies and his shortcomings.

Historically, whenever I felt exhausted and drained was when my inner bad girl screamed to come out and play. I knowingly made bad choices, mostly with exes, because I needed a release from the responsibilities I was drowning in. I loved feeling bad with them. I went for emotionally unavailable men because I was not emotionally available myself.

I yearned to not be the one in control, to feel sensual and free. to embrace my femininity and escape from survival mode.

I realized that I get turned on by desire. It makes me feel alive. With all of these men—especially the ones I danced with—their desire for me was sexy. They were dangerous. Exciting. They were not emotionally stable. In turn, I felt like they needed my strength. I brought out the best in them, and I brought out the worst in them. The residence I continued to take up in their minds left me satisfied. But I always had one foot out the door. That noose was forever hanging loosely around my neck, tightening anytime someone got too close. I saw a relationship as a prison from a young age, and I convinced myself I wanted no part of one. All I wanted was to be free. None of it was healthy. None of it translated to real love, companionship, or stability.

Taking ownership and acknowledging your strengths and shortcomings is crucial for growth. It was time for me to stop distracting myself with the devil and turn my focus to my business, my daughter, and finding a healthy partnership. I was ready.

Danika is the best thing that could have happened to me. She grounded me. She gave me roots. Since I gave birth, waking up to her every day is like Christmas morning. She's a gift. The best gift.

"Momma, we're gonna get a good, nice daddy one day."

"Yes, baby girl. We will."

Charlie ended the cycles of insecure men that I was attracting because subconsciously I was just as unavailable as they were. Somewhere inside I felt worthy to have healthy and secure relationships, even though chaos is what I knew. When this relationship ended I was done. I was choking with anxiety and stress from everything that was going on in my life which led me to surrender, healing, realizing I was enough for my daughter, falling in love with my soul. Realizing this was going to take a daily practice to embody this new woman, and this is where I decided to write this book. I felt I went through all of this not to keep it to myself. I want to help others, to let them know they are not alone. We are all growing, learning, finding our rhythm in this life.

8
THE LAST DANCE

"Be strong and courageous. Do not be afraid or terrified because of them, for the LORD your God goes with you; he will never leave you or forsake you."
(Deuteronomy 31:6)

I remember crying myself to sleep at eight years old, listening to my parents argue, the feeling that nothing is perfect, just accept your marriage slowly creeping in.

It's okay if you don't feel alive.

Years later I'd revisit those same feelings, sobbing over how hard Dave was on me. The distance between us. How he never made space for me in his closet when I moved in. How everything was about his family, his life...and I was just expected to adapt.

I never thought that years later, I would find myself pregnant and giving birth alone. By that point, I'd learned to put on a brave face. To only showcase strength to everyone around me. But alone,

I crumbled. I cried in the shower. I cried in my car. What felt like a nightmare would rear its head in reality as I woke up every morning to a growing belly. A growing belly that I longed to be kissed.

With Adam, and the men that followed, I found myself tangled in webs of men's games, lies, triangulation, and drama. I was exhausted. Confused. Lacking guidance and seeking love.

Each time I'd find strength to start over, another reminder of how lonely I was would begin to creep in. I arrived in Nashville with just my daughter, ready for a fresh start, only to encounter hateful eyes and ugly energy. Being banned and ostracized from the Honky Tonk and the area surrounding my studio invoked a new kind of loneliness. Not to mention, I'd never been so concerned for my life when entering an establishment. The sheer hate that flooded the room, from people who were complete strangers - it was unbearable.

And who did this hate come from? Church-goers sleeping with attached men. Locals who would be kind to your face, and gossip behind your back. The level of backstabbing and deceit was truly devastating, further exacerbating my already waning belief in the goodness of mankind. How could I stay strong, for myself and for my baby girl, in a place where everyone smiled to your face, while holding a knife to your back?

I buried the pain deep in my soul, the only way I've ever known how to cope. Appearing strong and confident, showing up like I had it all together was simply a beautiful mask for the pain, the memories, the scars seared into a little girl who never deserved them. A little girl who grew up to be a woman who only wanted to love and be loved.

I have danced with the devil. I looked him in the eyes. Those nights spent alone, protected by my walls, focusing on my career... it was the only thing that gave me a sense of control. I accepted being misunderstood for so long, pushing down the sensitivity and vulnerability, coating myself with a wall of armor. No one would ever break me down.

For years I've longed to shed that armor.

But when will it be safe?

9
TURTLE ISLAND

American Beauty Queen, Strong Warrior Goddess,
I am here. Lay down your arms.

American woman, let's go back to Turtle Island.

I was deep in my healing journey. I had surrendered. There was an awakening. My spirituality was ablaze. One day, in the midst of all this work, I turned to my friend Dawn and said, "I have done as much as I can at this point to heal myself as an individual. My next step is to be in a relationship."

When you put it out there, you shall receive.

Enter the Medicine Warrior.

I was working at the Country Music Awards. A group of friends were there tail-gating and they wanted me to go see a concert that night with everyone. As it turned out, they couldn't get enough tickets. I politely ducked out, knowing I had to work in the morning. They were insistent we at least have a drink before the show.

After I met up with them I decided to make my way towards my studio to dance a bit before heading home. I called my older friend Robert and asked him to meet me over at one of the Honky

Tonks. About a half hour into dancing, we took a break and took a seat near the front door.

Wade walked in the bar, head down, with his hat on. I automatically stood up and he looked at me. Robert introduced us, and as that happened, I was struck by a flash of light that crossed from the left to right side of my body. My mind went blank from that point, only recalling that we exchanged numbers. Strange, because I would never normally give my number out that quickly upon meeting someone.

He wasn't even supposed to be there that night. He was picking up a guitar strap from a vintage shop by my studio, and the owners and friends invited him out for a drink—something he rarely does.

I could feel his anxiety in the bar, and so I said, "You feel anxious, wanna get out of here? See my studio?" He said, "You can feel that."

We walked over to the studio and just talked all night, even continuing conversation in the car.

It all felt so comfortable, so familiar. I said to him, "I have met you before, I feel like I know you."

He kept staring at me, saying I resembled Lana Del Rey and noted that he loves her music. "Say Yes to Heaven" would end up being our song.

That Sunday we hung out for the first time. I went to visit him at his camper. He played songs for me, shared his life story. It was deep and intense, but there was also this instant connection between us. As he played, I could see these dark entities surrounding him, but I never felt scared of them.

We ended up hitting it off and continued to see each other. Shortly after meeting, the foundation of the camper became Turtle Island—a place that was secluded and surrounded by nature, allowing us to be fully present with each other. And in those moments, it was magic. We had so many different synchronicities.

First there was the flower petal. While I was spending the weekend with him at Turtle Island, Wade picked a flower for me, which I kept with me even when we jumped in the water. We were playing around, doing silly things like the lift from Dirty Dancing, when suddenly I noticed a petal had fallen off and floated to the water beside us. It was shaped like a heart.

Later that day we were out on the water on a Wave Runner, and mid-circle, it flipped. We went flying, our phones drowned in the water—it was a total mess. His friend Don came out to save the day. And in the middle of the chaos, as I'm trying to climb onto Don's Wave Runner, I noticed the flower he had picked floating beside me in the water. I scooped it up, and off we went to dry land. Back at the camper, recovering from the day, I looked down at the floor and once again saw the flower. It had somehow survived through all the chaos.

Knowing that it meant something, Wade kept the flower. He later made a necklace out of it for me, using a shadow box.

In the beginning it was those sort of connections that felt like they transcended space, time and reality. Because in those moments, they did. Everything there felt magical. We had no phones. We were submersed with nature, eating organic foods, cooking outside, playing in the water. There were boats and music and laughter and we both experienced heart openings that felt like a strange mix of ecstasy and agony. I could feel it in my chest, and at times it was so painful it actually scared me—like my heart was ripping open. He felt the same. With me, he felt like he had found his family. He felt full of love and confidence, and had a sense of home that he hadn't experienced since he was a six-year-old boy and his family broke apart.

One night we were laying in bed. I woke up and I saw this man standing on the other side of Wade. It looked like he had spikes going down his back. He looked straight forward, not at me, and I wasn't scared. It felt like he was protective of us. I went back to sleep, but couldn't get the image out of my mind.

I told Wade, and he seemed concerned. "That's not good, spikes indicates a lizard," he said.

"That's what I saw," I insisted.

A month later we went to his shop, where he wanted to show me some art work he had made. In it, there was this painting. It was a pregnant woman, with an Indian Chief facing her, holding her hands. He had feathers running down his back. Oh my God, that is what I saw, I thought. It wasn't spikes. It was feathers. I saw what he had painted, years before he met me.

But all of these amazing connections and synchronicities sadly weren't enough to sustain Wade and me in the real world. After about three months of having this wonderful relationship, his insecurities started to come out. It became very intense. He would have angry outbursts over seemingly small things, like when he flipped out about items in my cupboard not being organic after spending time with a friend of mine on some house work. It was bizarre how a switch just flipped, and suddenly this kind, gentle, loving man was so incredibly angry. As his insecurities started to come through more and more, I could feel him projecting them onto me.

I was so confused. He was crumbling, and there was nothing I could do to stop it, because for some reason unbeknownst to me, I held the hammer that was breaking this man down. Things I shared in moments of vulnerability now became evidence of reasons why we shouldn't be together. He brought up exes, my successes, my daughter, grasping for every reason under the sun why we wouldn't work—are we starting to see a pattern?

Because I sure as hell was. And this time, things were going to be different. It hit me. I had enough. I had to let this man go. I loved him enough to know I had to set him free.

The turning point came in the midst of yet another argument, when he said, "I don't want to hurt you or Danika."

"Then leave us alone."

That was it. It was no longer about needing a rich man, or a someone at my vibration, or someone stable—I needed a man who had done the work. And Wade clearly had not.

More things started to unfold after that moment—like yet another ex lingering in the background of his life—and more psychological warfare that kept the 'are we/aren't we' dance going on far longer than it should. But at the end of the day, it all came down to this:

When I started writing this book, I was healing. I had closed all of these chapters on toxic men. Then I met Wade, thinking, this one will be different.

I was right. It was different. Wade and I broke up because we had to break up. It wasn't because of his past, or because of cheating or lying or narcissistic abuse. It was one of the hardest relationship endings I experienced because there wasn't a clear cut reason.

Logically my mind knows, move on, move forward. Even my heart is saying, "Be open to someone new." But there's still a tiny string attached to him in my chest, and no matter what I do, or how hard I pray, I can't seem to be released from it.

In the midst of our break up he would say to me, "I want my heart back."

And I get it now. I do too. Because what we had at Turtle Island was so real. It wasn't love bombing. It wasn't summertime or a first time, or any of those clichés. It was deep and spiritual—like heaven on earth. What it used to be back in the day without phones, without social media, without bullshit. It was about what matters —eating organic, family, fishing, hunting, having fun, enjoying life and music and this beautiful, spiritual, loving connection. We both experienced something that many people never encounter in their lives. It imprints you.

What I'm the most grateful about my time with Wade is that it brought me back full circle to my authentic self. Now I have these boundaries that I haven't had since I was twenty years old and my Nan and my father used to tell me, "Elizabeth, never take shit from a man."

When I was in my twenties, and even throughout my thirties, there was this explosive dichotomy of not wanting to take that shit but also giving myself over and over again to the wrong people. Affair after affair with the wrong man, not regulating more carefully who I allowed into my life and my body. But now I'm back to a place where my womb is sacred. I don't need to just hook up, I don't need to have sex to fill my needs. My needs are fulfilled within myself, I will be practicing celibacy till I meet my husband. I'm not exchanging energy and not giving someone myself anymore. I'm done.

It's okay that Wade and I didn't work out. Mirroring and triggering was our rhythm. It wasn't in alignment. Not only did he bring me back to my authentic self, but I became my authentic self with him. He didn't fall in love with Liz the dancer, or the businesswoman. He fell in love with my soul—and I his—which is why there are no hard feelings, despite the pain of letting this connection go. My boundaries are firm. The only way to see someone's true colors is to see how they respond to them. This applies to every relationship—romantic, family, friends, and work.

If they respond well to those boundaries, amazing. We're in alignment to move forward. If not, that's okay too. No hard feelings. We go our separate ways. It has run its course. I surrender to the fact that those boundaries are my barometer, and in practicing life in this new way, people show more respect.

I am back. I went full circle. I came back to my authentic self.

I realized every heartache and let down turned into my personal turning point and evolution.

I remember waking up with a vision one morning. There was the divine masculine on the left facing the divine feminine on the right with space in between them, and a string coming from both of their chests going upwards to an angel who was orchestrating the strings. Earth was under them, and it looked like the Garden of Eden. The vision and message I was receiving was the two souls being orchestrated from the divine to bring their love to heal this world and bring heaven back to earth. I asked Danika to draw this picture for me cause she loves drawing. I drew it out as well and sent it to Tina, my tattoo artist, to sketch it for me.

Thank you, Divine Masculine, for triggering me. Empowering me and taking me to GOD. To be rid of breaking my ego and the illusion of the three dimensional world. Refocusing my energy back on myself. To help me ascend on my journey to be the better version of myself. Thank you. No one has done that for me.

❧❧

A man and a woman stand facing each other, their souls connected by a string orchestrated by the divine angel above. The power of the angel's divine love heals the Earth and creates the New Earth where Heaven exists on Earth filled with colorful plants, beautiful trees, animals and people, all thriving together. Hate and Evil did not win.

❧❧

10
BEGIN AGAIN

Valentine's Day, 2023. The day I realized my love for my daughter is enough.

Ever since my pregnancy, I overcompensated for the lack of a father's presence for Danika. I thought if I met someone while she was young, she wouldn't know life without one. Time after time, as I tried to seek and make up for what I felt Danika needed, I was drawn to the wrong men. It turns out, all the love she needed was right there, in me, all along.

I remember there was a blizzard the day she was born. Wind roared through the vents of the hospital, the rest of the floor echoing in the emptiness. After my epidural, my doctor sat down with me, wanting to know my story. As my epidural kicked in, I said, "How I feel about her father, is how I feel about my legs—numb." She told me, "You have all the love this child will need."

Almost five years later, I finally get it. I feel enough for my child. One night, a few months ago, she said, "Mommy, cuddle me tight and don't let me go." Ironically, this is what I say to her!

When it's the right time, the right one will come in to complement and add to our love, not complete it nor take from it.

It's been a wild ride so far. There are choices I could have made differently, but if I had, I wouldn't be me and I wouldn't have lived this full, enriched life. I definitely wouldn't have my baby girl.

Every obstacle, letdown, roadblock, setback, those telling me to get a real job, be normal ... it all just pushed me to have the fire to persevere. I'm grateful for all of it, because it taught me grace, humility, strength, and confidence.

There was an absence of warmth and compassion growing up. I was never a daddy's girl. My childhood was different. Now I look at my daughter, and I long to not have to exist in my masculine survival mode much longer. I dream of the day I can live in my feminine self and be a mom to my daughter, and not have to be a father as well.

I've learned to forgive my parents, and to forgive these men. My parents did the best they could with what they knew from their upbringing and lessons within life.

Those men have inner battles they fight. Their actions towards me had everything to do with that and are not a reflection on me or my self-worth. I am blessed with a wonderful family and beautiful love affairs. I've moved forward with peace, surrender, and grace.

I'm still growing, strengthening my true essence, and creating healthy, secure habits and boundaries to keep this new, beautiful person on her highest path.

The best advice I can offer is to never give another person power. Power over your emotions, your daily activities, your mental state, your confidence, your value. No one but God is the righteous one. We are love and must be love. We are all special in our own way. Own that, walk with that, and everything else will fall into place.

Surrender.

If you want something, you will get it. Stay the course, be tenacious and know exactly what it is you want. You will have many obstacles. Break through them, take the lesson, apply it in the next step, and keep the fire lit as you crush and dance through.

Listen.

Watch.

Take it in.

Analyze.

And move accordingly.

Some things are not meant for you and some are just a matter of timing. The lessons are important to reach the blessings.

I promise what waits for you on the other side of those lessons is beautiful. It's divine. And it will heal you in a way that only a true medicine warrior can, unlocking your inner wolf, your inner goddess, and allowing love to flow freely between you, around you, and within you.

You are love.

Surrender.

EPILOGUE

After my divorce from Mark, I created Country Fusion.

❧

Dave brought me to Jersey where I built Country Fusion and met amazing friends. That led me to Adam who gave me Danika.

❧

From Andrew I learned crazy and toxic chemistry, and what red flags are.

❧

Tim gave me the push to Nashville.

❧

Charlie gave me the "It's time to write this book."

❧

Wade completed the circle which brought me back to me— my true self—that girl I was before I got married and all these relationships.

This Valentine's Day in 2024 right before publishing this book, Danika asked, "Momma, is Valentine's Day like Mother's Day?"

"No, Valentine's is about hearts and love and Mother's Day is for moms that had babies like you're my baby."

"Would be funny if there was a dad's day," she replied. I knew where we were going and tears started filling my eyes. I told her there is it's called Father's Day. She said, "Well, I don't have a dad so I can't celebrate it."

"Uncle Matt just became a dad and we have Pa," I answered, knowing that wouldn't be enough.

"Yeah, but they are not my dad."

The tears started flowing. I said, "I know, and I am so sorry baby. But I love you so, so much."

"Will we have a dad one day?"

"Yes, we most certainly will."

"What's his name?"

I laughed. "I don't know yet but I have to start interviewing and it's going to take me some time. Maybe he will have a son or daughter and you can get a sister or a brother too."

She thought about this, then replied, "But not a mom cause I have you. Just the boys."

"Yes," I said, with another laugh.

I know my path was to go through this, and she chose me to be her mom. My past has no access to me any longer. The future is bright with possibilities. Head up, shoulders back, Danika's hand in mine as we walk forward, protected and guided from above through surrendering to the process.

"The Art of Surrender"
Your way home to your authentic self.

I am enough!

I feel so loved.
I feel ready for love.
I feel ready to meet my person.
I am love.
I have boundaries.
My womb is scared.
I am sacred.
I vibrate highly.
I attract high vibrational.
I manifest high vibrational.
I will have a masculine who adores us.
I will have a family.
I forgive myself.
I forgive others.
I had to learn.
I had to grow.
I had to heal.
I am ready.
I will be successful in love, health, commitment,
family, work, money, and friends.

I am enough!

About the Author

Elizabeth Mooney lives with her daughter, Danika, in the Nashville area. She writes about her journey of self-reliance and love with the hope that others will read her story and compare it to their own lives.

Love for yourself must reside inside you before you can love another. And the same is true for the person you think you love. If they show you they don't love themselves, then they cannot truly love you.

Acknowledgments

My mom, Christine, for her love and support, her selflessness and warmth over the years.

My dad, Tom, for being a constant presence with guidance from a logical and clear standpoint.

My daughter, Danika, and fur babies, Kimba and Chance, who gave me the strength to never give up and the love that I forever needed.

My friend, Tina Sulano, a talented tattoo artist who did the cover artwork for this book.

My friends, so many wonderful friends I have. For their time, their energy, their love, their laughs, their help, support, my cheerleaders, my rock. I have so many beautiful people around me: Dawn, Roe Roe, Ronnie, Jean, and Suzi.

My brothers, Thomas and Matthew, thank you for being father figures to Danika and making us all laugh.

My grandparents—Nana Vera and Pa Joe—for their love, strength, teachings, and fond memories as a child. Poppy, thank you for your warmth, love and big smile, always feeling safe in your presence.

My clients and instructors. Country Fusion wouldn't be what it is if it weren't for you. To believe in me, see the vision, love it, spread the love, and to keep it alive.

I'd also like to thank my publisher, editor, and graphic designer, Valerie Connelly, for all the professional design advice and guidance she provided throughout the process of creating this book.

Elizabeth Mooney

Printed in the USA
CPSIA information can be obtained
at www.ICGtesting.com
JSHW070332280324
60087JS00009B/25

9 781945 257476